Do Dope Shit

OTHER BOOKS BY ROBERT M. DRAKE

For Excerpts and Updates please follow:

Instagram.com/rmdrk
Facebook.com/rmdrk
Twitter.com/rmdrk

ISBN: 978-0-9986293-6-0

Book Cover: Robert M. Drake
Cover Image licensed by Shutter Stock Inc.

For Sevyn, For Summer

All my words are yours.
All of my words, will always be yours.

CONTENTS

DEAD POP ART

ROBERT M. DRAKE

NO ONE IS

No one is ever really gone.

Everyone you love
is with you

and you will always
remember them
as you once did.

In what hurts
and what brings you laughter.

All together.
All the time.

WITH ME

With me
you do not have to pretend.

You can be
who you want to be

and you can share yourself
the best way you know how.

We can ignore our scars
and not remind ourselves
of our past.

We can love right now
and none of it has to be

right or wrong.

It just has to be
enough

to make us ignore

everything
that hurts.

BY MYSELF

And every night

I find myself

laying on my bed,
staring at the ceiling
and thinking:

"Does any of this
really, matter?

Is any of this real?"

The days are pulled
into other days

and the nights
step into the day.

And it all cycles.
It all collapses

into my arms.

And I miss you
and you are not here.

And I try to keep going.

And I continue to swim.

And the current gets
the best of me every time.

And sometimes I drown
while other times

I barely make it
to the shore.

And it hurts
because it's supposed to

hurt.

And I can't seem
to wrap my finger on it.

And it hurts even more
when I do.

And sometimes
nothing makes any sense.

And all I really want

is for you…

to come back home.

I DO NOT KNOW

I don't know you
but all of this feels
too familiar.

This ache.

This longing to be held.

Somewhere
in those big brown eyes
of yours.…

I catch more than just
feelings.

More than just life
and death.

Somewhere in you…
there is a place.

And it is the only place
that keeps me warm.

The only place
I can breathe

but also,

the only place

I can never seem
to find.

SOME WILL BE TRUE

Not everything
is what it seems,

and not everything
people say will be true.

Although,
at first,

words may seem pretty
or comforting.

Some people will make you
care for them.

They will make you
trust them

and even fall in love
with them.

And once you do,
soon enough,

the truth will emerge...
because it always does.

One way or another.

People can never run
too far from their true intentions.

They can never hold in
their true colors

or what they feel
and think...

and to be honest,
some people are just assholes.

Some will take you
for granted
and some will betray you

in the worse of ways.

And it will hurt.

It will break your spirit
and make you feel

as if

you're the smallest person
in the world.

But you will learn
from these little tragedies

and you will get through them
as well.

And the more you hurt,
the more you'll learn
how to properly protect

your fucking heart.

And the more you break,
the stronger you'll get,

and the more you meet
shitty people...

the easier it gets
to keep the ones
who make you feel free.

So that's the point,
to get hurt a few times here
and there,

to fall into people's bullshit
every once in a while.

It's bound to happen...

there's no way around it
and there's no other way to learn,
to grow and heal.

So if it hurts...

it is only because it must.

So live,
learn from experience
and remember

how some people are cancerous
but not all of them
are meant to destroy you.

The goal is to find the ones
who will walk with you,

side by side
to make a difference.

And that's the realist shit
you can do.

You can learn from the ones
who bring pain

and learn to keep the ones
who give love—

close...

no matter what
you do.

Keep the ones who love
and practice love.

All else means nothing.
All else

isn't strong enough
to move

a grain of sand.

SHE IS GONE

And when she is gone
you will remember

all the things
you should have said.

All the things
you should have done.

You will remember
everything you ignored

and it will eat you alive

because

you had the chance
to but didn't take

the opportunities
to show her

how you feel.

TWO BIRDS

You're a bird

and you don't need
a pair of wings

to tell you who you are.

The same way
you don't need a lover

to make you feel
as if

your *heart is free*.

OPEN HEART

You do not
have to close your heart

because someone hurt you.

The past does not
have to be so bitter
on the future.

So look around you,
open your eyes.

There are so *many* people
who need your love.

THE GIFT AND CURSE

It's a gift and a curse.

You meet someone.
You fall in love with them.

Create beautiful memories,
and in the end,

all you're left with
is an empty heart.

And sometimes
you get over it
and heal

while other times...

you don't.

YOU ARE BEAUTIFUL

You're beautiful

not because
you have a pretty face

but because
the chaos stirs around you
and still,

you choose to love
everyone the same.

You take tragedies
and turn them into gold.

You know how others feel
and you give the people around you

all the reasons
they need

to believe in love again.

And that's what makes you
so goddamn beautiful.

INSTANT LIVES

And in an instant

I found myself wondering
if I was ever

going to be able
to see you again.

If I was ever
going to recover

from the wounds
I greeted during our hello.

And I sit back
and inhale…

full of sadness
and a heart full of glass.

This *must be*
what it feels like

to be in love.

STOP THIS NOW

Maybe you should stop
overthinking so much

and trust the way
life happens.

Things change.

Every year you grow
into someone else.

Every year you have
the opportunity
to start over and begin.

To rise and face the world
the way you want to.

Take this with you,
you *beautiful* human being...

don't be afraid to fail.
Don't be afraid to fall.

Don't be afraid
to get your heart broken,

don't be afraid at all.

The fear is in your head.
The doubt is in your heart.

And regret survives in the memory
that is, if you feed it—if you
give into it.

So please,
before you go…

overthinking is a self-inflicting act.
It is the suicide, the doubt of self,

the tragedy no one understands.

It is *instant* death
without lifting

a single sword.

Don't give into it
you know you are

stronger
than that

and capable of
so much more.

NEVER NEVER

You must never forget
to chase

all the things
that make you feel free.

HOW IT FEELS

And I know
how it feels...

to be surrounded
by the people you love

and yet,
still feel completely alone.

Still feel
as if something is missing.

My dear,
when will you learn...

you are not empty.
You are full.

It is just,
you have yet
to discover

that the war in your head
is over.

That the brokenness
you feel in your heart
is a *lie*

and everything
that makes you beautiful
is real.

Because you are real, baby.
Your heart is real.

What you feel is real.

It's just sometimes
your mind plays tricks on you.

That's all.

DO NOT TELL ME

Don't tell me
it doesn't matter anymore.

Because your scars
are more than just scars.

Your scars represent
the times you almost
lost your heart.

The times you almost
lost your *goddamn mind.*

Your goddamn voice,
soul and hope.

Don't tell me
it was all for nothing.

It is all for something,
always,

and you should never
forget

how far you've come.

MOVING ON

I'm moving on
and by doing so,

I am accepting
how things will never be
the same.

How the things
I feel toward you

are meant for someone else.

And how
the first two things

are things
I should have done
and realized a lot sooner.

This is my truth
and I'm letting you go,

and I'm sure people
who feel the same way

are doing it too.

IT IS REAL

If it's real
they won't let you go

and if it's meant
to be

they'll follow you
no matter how far
you go.

ALL THE REASONS

The only reason it hurts
is because
I still love you.

And the only reason
I can't forget you

is because
moving on is hard

and there are too many reasons
reminding me

of why letting you

go

is even *harder.*

SAVE YOU TONIGHT

Your heart is broken
and there isn't a person

in the world
that could help you...

to make you forget.

And some will say
to move on,

while others will say
to just keep yourself busy.

But nothing seems to change
when your heart aches.

Nothing seems to move.

And sadly,
there's no cure
for what you feel

except time
and time
and more time.

You have to give yourself

the right amount of time

to move on

and that's something
only you

would know how long
it would take.

Stay beautiful.

NOTHING ELSE

If nothing else,
just remember

how one day
you will find someone

and you will feel
what I once felt for you.

And you will remember me
and you will think:

*"I now understand
and I wish I wouldn't have hurt you
the way I did.*

I'm sorry."

I hope you remember that
and make peace

with all
that you have done
and caused.

SOMEWHERE

It is sad to say,
but somewhere

between who we were
and who we are now

there's a lonely place…

where ghosts whisper
and relive

what we once had.

Damn.

NOT SURE WHO I AM

And now
you're with someone else

and I'm not sure
what to feel.

I'm not sure
how to hurt.

How to live.
How to spend my time.

Shit.
Fuck.
Damnit.

The body turns cold.
The mind stays relentless.
And the heart remains empty.

And all I know

is

that I have to
figure out how to heal
on my own.

How to move on
on my own.

How to figure out
what to live…

and understand
what it is

I must do
with all my broken parts

after a lifetime
spent

with you.

STICKS AND STONES

Because sticks
and stones

may break your bones
but it takes

just a few words
to break a human heart.

MY OWN SPACE

I need my own space,
but all space without you

is empty.

And all space
without us is
meaningless.

Sometimes

I want to be alone
because I feel alone

but the stars within me
need you to breathe,

to expand even further.

And what hurts is,
how I could never tell
if you're loving me

or if I am loving you.

If I'm chasing you
or if you're chasing me.

This love of ours
sometimes makes me feel alone

but *everything* is empty
without you.

NOT MAGIC, NO

It's not magic.

It's chemicals in our brains
telling us what to feel.

Telling us
what we should
or shouldn't love.

So if that's what it is
then I don't want it
any other way.

*I love you
with all mind,
all soul*

and cross my heart
and hope to die…

hold my hand,
lay next to me

and do not say a word.

I wouldn't want to live
any other way.

NEW NEW NEW

New dreams.
New realities.
New memories.

Nothing lasts
but nothing is lost.

We take who we share
a life with—with us

and never
do we forget

the way they once
made us feel.

Miss you, my brother…
not a day goes by

when I do not think
of your smile.

NOT HERE BUT WHERE

And you're no longer here.

And I just hope
where ever you've gone...

you've found the courage
to say what you feel.

To do
what you want to do

and to become
who you've always wanted
to become.

The sun keeps shining
and everything around me

reminds me
of your laughter.

It's a good time
to be alive, kiddo…

it truly is

but everything feels wrong
without you.

Everything feels different.

I just hope you're happy
and I hope wherever

*you've gone
you feel free.*

ALWAYS THE PROBLEM

And that's the problem,
you think you have to
apologize for what you feel.

You think you have to
be careful with what you say
or who you want to be.

Well I say,
fuck anyone
who makes you feel
any different.

Fuck anyone
who makes you feel small,

and fuck anyone
who makes you feel

as if

the love you carry within
is wrong.

Because it's not.
None of it is.

So choose you,

choose love,

and choose the people
who stand for something,

and make a difference
because you were born to do so.

You are here
to set things on fire

and set them free.

LATE NIGHT PROSE

It was late
and we had a couple
of drinks in us.

She told me
she was rebuilding herself.

That she was...
trying to run away
from her past.

That no matter what she did,
everytime he would need her

she would go running back to him.

She told me
he would mistreat her.

That he would ignore her
and only want to spend time

with her
when he needed something
from her.

And when she asked me
what I thought, again.

(this has been going on for years.)

Because she only comes to me
when she feels broken.

When she feels alone and cold.

I took another sip of my vodka.

I looked at her
and said,

"Maybe he does love you.
Maybe he really does,

who knows
but he doesn't show it
how he's supposed to.

He doesn't look for you
when you've gone missing.

And he doesn't comfort you
when you feel most alone.

It's sad, it really is...
because forever

is a long time
to chase someone
you know you don't deserve."

She smiled as if I were wrong
and she was too embarrassed
to tell me I was wrong.

And I smiled back

because I knew,
she knew,

she was well aware
that she deserved
so much more.

BURY THIS IN YOUR MIND

You must keep this in mind.

The people who hurt you,
only hurt you

because they believe
with their hearts

that they are allowed to hurt
the people who love them.

So you don't have to
find ways to justify it

because you're embarrassed
or ashamed that you keep believing

in their lies,
that you keep letting them in.

And yes,
sometimes people change
but sometimes they don't,

not unless they've lost
something valuable to them.

Something that hurts.

So cry,
and cry because it's okay
to do so.

Sooner or later
they'll realize your worth.

They'll realize
what they've lost.

Because that's how things happen.
That's how people change.

How people learn to appreciate
other people.

So break apart
it's okay to do so.

Cry a little
it's good for the soul

and know
the cycle of things.

What comes around
goes around,

and those who hurt you
have yet,

to get hurt themselves.

That's just the way
things are.

DO NOT SHAKE YOUR VOICE

Don't feel discouraged.

It takes years
to find your own voice,

to realize your worth
and to know what you deserve.

It takes years of pain,
disappointment
and struggle

to understand
how important you are.

It takes years,
my love,
and many of them.

So live
and do so, courageously.

Face the world bravely
and carry the love you have

within your heart
with no fear.

And don't forget to dance.
Don't forget to smile
and laugh...

because it is the little things
in life

that make it
worthwhile.

LET GO

Let go of anyone
and anything

that makes you believe
that you are not

worthy of love.

OPEN UP

You open
yourself to people

and yet
no one gets
what you're saying.

No one feels it.
No one relates to it.

Well,
that's okay

maybe you're not meant
to be understood.

Maybe you're not meant
to be broken down

and categorized.

You're wild, baby.
You're free.

And like a wild animal
emerging from the ocean
you're too strong
to be ignored.

You set the whole
goddamn stage on fire.

Maybe standing out

is what makes you
who you are.

ATTENTION!

You think attention is love.

You think controlling someone
means you care.

You think hearing
but not listening

means you're understanding.

When will you learn?
Will it ever stop?

Will it ever begin?
If you don't love her,
then leave her.

Let her find someone
who can fuel her fire.

Let her be.

And the same goes for you.
Take time on yourself.

Appreciate and learn
about yourself.

Discover what matters most,
start anew
and leave everything that hurts behind.

These are my words of wisdom.

Love yourself
then love someone else.

Only then
will you know
how to give your love

to a woman who
genuinely deserves it.

OVER SOMEONE

Getting over someone
is hard

but I promise you
the outcome is worth it.

You'll learn new things
about yourself.

Like how to let go,
why to let go

and when to let go.

You'll develop new characteristics.
New outcomes.

New solutions to your problems.

And believe me,
the growth will be beautiful.

It will be worth
all the stars in people's eyes.

I promise.

HELLO GOOD-BYE

And after the last good-bye
you're never quite the same.

And as the years pass,
the harder it is
to find love.

And some days
you feel everything,

as if your deepest wounds
are on fire.

And the words

"Don't leave"

cling on the tip
of your tongue.

And if it hurts,
it is only because
you *still* care.

And the world keeps going
but everything within reach
is completely still.

And some nights
you feel more alone.

And everyone around you
wants to understand

but you don't have the words
to express what you feel.

Getting over someone
is never easy.

It hurts
and believe me,

it's going to be hard
but don't lose hope.

Don't lose
that last piece of yourself.

Don't let your brokenness
define you—control you.

People leave.

They become storms—
breaking your windows

and tearing down your walls
but that doesn't mean

it's the end.

That doesn't mean
you have to submerge yourself
in the water.

People leave,
they must,

it's what they do
but you're strong

and you've been here before.

So cry,
it's okay...

I'm here with you.

Just remember,
the ones who hurt you

will one day
seek you

and you will be
a different person.

You will forgive them.

You will move on,

and you will accept the way
things used to hurt

but you will

never

let it define you
for who you are.

Amen.

EMOTIONAL BEING

You're emotional.

Therefore,
of course,

you're going to overreact sometimes.

Of course,
you're going to speak your mind
without thinking twice.

You feel too much
and that's not necessarily a bad thing.

You have a heart
and it loves so much

that you barely know
how to control it

at all.

ABOUT LOVE

That's the thing about love.

You never know
when to give up.

You never know
when to let go,

no matter how broken
your hearts is.

Sometimes,
you will put yourself last

no matter how bad
it hurts.

THIS DAY

The day you accept
yourself for who you are—

flaws and all...

is the moment
nothing and no one

can bother you.

You are your own killer
and there is nothing worse

than not believing
in yourself.

LIST OF PROBLEMS

You say you have a problem.

That you have too much love
but you have no one to give it to.

But that's not the *real* problem.

The *real* problem is,
that yes,

you do have too much love
but you're too damn busy

trying to give it
to the people who don't deserve it.

To the people
who don't care.

To the people
who think you'll always be around

but don't give you the time
you need,

the affection you want.

You're too damn busy,

and that's the keyword here.

You're too busy
giving pieces of yourself

to other people,
rather than giving them to yourself.

And that's the tragedy here.

You give
and you give
and you give

until there's nothing left.

Until your heart is empty
and your soul is starved
of love.

But that's not
the core of your problems.

That's not
what's going to kill you

in the end.

The truth is,
no one is going to love you

not unless
you love yourself.

And no one
is going to see you

for who you are
not unless
you see yourself first.

You have to love yourself
before you love another person.

You have to know yourself,
be in love with yourself...

and it works both ways.

You receive
what you give

and you give
what you receive

and there has never
been a flaw

in that.

I AM...

I am ready
to be held.

To be kissed
and touched.

So believe me
when I say

I won't go away...
it is not in my nature

to leave
the people I love.

STAY AWAY

Stay away
from anyone

who makes you question
your fire

and don't give in
to the bullshit.

You are
who you are

no matter how many times
your world

has burned.

AND NOW

And now

looking back at things
and after all these years.

My heart still aches
and it's not because

you're gone
but because

I spent so much time
loving you.

So much time
trying to make things work.

And it hurts
because it's time I wasted.

Time
I know
I'll never get back.

Time I could have spent
on myself.

Time…

I could have spent
on the people

I love.

DO NOT QUESTION THIS

The best moments
in your life

are the ones
shared with the people
you love.

Never question that fact.
It is what it is.

Enjoy.

WITHOUT WORDS

Without words,
or some kind of interaction…

when it's over
it's over.

It's one of those things
you just know

and not one of those things
you learn.

CHANGE WHAT YOU SEE

Go all the way with it.

Whether it be
someone you want to love.

Something you believe in
or a change you want to see.

Go all the way with it.

It might take longer
than you think.

Maybe a week,
a month,

a year
or even a decade

but don't give up.

Give in.
Do it from within.

Always from within.

From the core
of your soul

and heart.

Go all the way with it.

Even if you lose yourself.
If you lose a part of your soul.

Don't lose sight
of what you love.

Of what you want
to do or be.

Go all the way with it.

And do it,
even if it kills you.

We all need something
worth dying for.

Chasing it
is what makes

this lifetime
beautiful.

HURTING NOW

And I'm still hurting
over the people

who've left
without saying good-bye

and the words
I've said

that have gone
unheard.

If I loved you
and you're no longer here,
then,

I still love you
and sadly,

everything feels
like the last night I saw you,

right before you walked away.

And if that's not love

then I don't want to know
what it is.

The truth is,
I'm still grieving

and I'm still breaking my bones
over the people

I've lost.

Over the people
who are no longer here.

LOVE YOU

Let people love you,
there's nothing beautiful

or holy
about feeling alone.

About feeling empty
and above all,

about thinking
no one is out there

for you.

NEVER THOUGHT

I never thought
losing someone

would make me appreciate life
so much.

And I never knew
I had love in me

until

I watched
the only person I needed
walk away.

PART OF ME

A part of me wants you.

But I only know
how to love intensely

and I want to love you,
genuinely,

I do
but I don't know what to do

with another
human heart.

I don't know how to care
for it.

How to water it.

I am lost,
confused, crazy,

drunk in love.

Dumb and full
of contradiction.

A part of me wants

to love you

but the other part
is telling me

to stay
the *hell away.*

HOLDING YOU

I will hold you
when you have the urge
to fall apart

and I will love you
and give you

all that I am
when you feel

like you've got
nothing left to give.

That's my word.

THE MOON

And tonight

I will give you the moon.

I will whisper
into your ear

and make you forget

anyone
and everyone

who has ever
loved you

the wrong way.